THE MYSTERY OF BEING:
THE PRESENCE AND ABSENCE OF GOD

THE MYSTERY OF BEING

The Presence and Absence of God

JAMES O'CONNELL

VERITAS

First published 2009 by
Veritas Publications
7/8 Lower Abbey Street
Dublin 1
Ireland
Email publications@veritas.ie
Website www.veritas.ie

ISBN 978 1 84730 194 9

A catalogue record for this book is available from the British Library.

The lines from 'The Great Hunger' by Patrick Kavanagh are reprinted from
Collected Poems, edited by Antoinette Quinn (Allen Lane, 2004), by kind permission
of the Trustees of the Estate of the late Katherine B. Kavanagh,
through the Jonathan Williams Literary Agency.
Scripture quotations taken from the New Revised Standard Version Bible,
copyright © 2006 by the National Council of the Churches of Christ
in the United States of America.

Designed by Barbara Croatto
Printed in the Republic of Ireland by ColourBooks Ltd, Dublin

CONTENTS

INTRODUCTION

This book on understanding God is intended for people who have accepted a belief in God and a relationship with him[1] and who wish to deepen their knowledge and strengthen that relationship. It is also written for those of an agnostic outlook who wish to reflect further on human origins, ethos and destiny. In a narrower sense it is written for teachers of religion in schools as well as for those who study theology or preach in churches and elsewhere.

Many Christians, in moving through a secular education in the arts or sciences and in growing through life experiences, have begun to realise that the understanding of God that they have taken with them from primary school or Church instructions is no longer adequate and needs to be refined. But they cannot readily lay their hands on material that would offer purified concepts and avoid images drawn excessively from a folk past.

Also, at a time when many proponents of atheism – the best known in the English-speaking world is Richard Dawkins – are no longer content just to deny the existence of God but wish to convince others of the non-existence of the deity, believers need to be able to weigh the worth of the negative arguments and to suggest their inadequacy.

If we accept that God is love and we are called to love in return, in any such relationship we, lovers, seek to deepen our understanding of God and one another. If we are to love God and draw closer to him, we need to come to know him more profoundly so as to relate better to him. Many of us may indeed join with St Augustine who lamented in Book X of his *Confessions*: 'Too late have I loved you, ever old and ever new! Too late have I loved you.' Love has to be worked on, and worked for, all our lives; and in loving God and one another we grow in love.

The three chapters that follow this introduction are arranged around three different approaches to the understanding of God. There is, first, the approach of reason to God: the God of the philosophers. The second chapter deals with the God of the Jews: the Abrahamic tradition. Third, a set of reflections explores belief in the God and Father of Jesus Christ: the Christian tradition.

In beginning this short study with the role of reason in discerning the nature of God, the being who exists of himself without the intervention of any other being, I am making a fundamental point. While few persons would come to know and fewer still would die for a cerebral God of the philosophers, reason is nevertheless our principal instrument in reflecting on the Judaeo-Christian scriptures and traditions. Not least, it is the instrument through which we bring the riches both of historical learning and contemporary experience to bear on the understanding of God. A God of revelation who flouted the rules of reason would be a God involved in contradictions between his work of creation and his Son's work of atonement. In that sense there must always be a primacy of reason.

A God of faith who has become known through the faith and worship of the Jews is richer and more accessible than the God of reason. He reaches beyond the ranks of the philosophers to touch the great bulk of the simple and ordinary members of humankind. Yet this God of the Jewish faith did not spring readymade from early Jewish reflection and worship but came from long centuries of intellectual searching and purification. There are, for example, almost certainly centuries between the two accounts of creation in the first and second chapters of Genesis. In one account the Adam story is almost crudely anthropomorphic and draws powerfully on a folklorist tradition, and in the other account there is a sophisticated rendering of beginnings that has as its backdrop the priestly worship of the temple. I have mostly emphasised the later part of the Jewish scriptures. But it is crucial to understand – something that the opponents of theism often get as wrong as Christian fundamentalists – that the Bible is not one book but a collection of documents put together from different periods of time and that describe an evolution of thought, ethics and ritual. The Jewish writers, priests, elders and prophets who cherished and leavened their people collaborated with one another over long years to create and to bequeath to posterity one of the great religious legacies of history.

The Christian scriptures and tradition are saturated with the history, ritual and thought of the Jewish people. Christ undertook his mission of atonement (at-one-ment) at a moment when the Jewish religious tradition, especially in the later prophets, had reached a high degree of development. He could speak to an audience that was ready for the further teaching that he was imparting; and he could gather followers who would appreciate – and in many cases follow literally – the example of the sacrifice of his life that he gave. He turned out to be a messiah different from what most had expected. He not only acted to prepare a kingdom of truth and justice but he taught with authority and revealed in his life a concept of a God who came close to humans and who was full of love and compassion. Paul, one of his most learned and passionate disciples, summed up the gift that Christ brought: '… but you have received a spirit of adoption. When we cry "Abba! Father", it is that very Spirit bearing witness with our spirit that we are children of God, and if children, then heirs, heirs of God and joint heirs with Christ …' (Rom 8:15-17).

Finally, in considering the God of the philosophers, the God of the Jews, and the God and Father of Jesus Christ, I have limited myself to reflecting in a relatively simple way on the nature and the work of God. For that reason I have only begun to do justice to the complexity of natural theology, to the varied riches of the Hebrew scriptures, to the wonderful analyses and images of the Christian scriptures, and to the primordial descriptions of the person of Jesus in the gospels. I hope that this small study will be for my readers a continuation of their own search.

NOTE

1 I am accepting the convention of using the masculine pronoun for God. But no matter what conventions particular cultures have historically adopted, the divinity is no more male than it is female, and we can no better call God father than mother.

I

THE GOD OF THE PHILOSOPHERS

HERE I AM, MY END AND MY MEANING!
I CALL YOU … NO, IT IS YOU WHO CALL ME TO YOU.
HALLAJ, QASIDA I (DIWAN)

A fundamental element in our human experience is the understanding that we have come about in an utterly contingent[1] and accidental way. Even if other things did not remind us, the chance encounters that led our parents to one another and prompted the act of generation that gave us biological being reminds us that our existence owes nothing to ourselves. We are in our most personal and thinking terms upthrusts from nothingness and products of accident. Pascal with his literary genius catches the sense of human contingency:

> When I consider the short duration of my life, swallowed up in the eternity before and after, the little space which I fill, and even can see, engulfed in the infinite immensity of spaces of which I am ignorant, and which know me not,

I am frightened, and am astonished at being here rather than there; for there is no reason why here rather than there, why now rather than then. Who has put me here? By whose order and direction have this place and time been allotted to me? ...The eternal silence of these infinite spaces frightens me.[2]

Yet because we think creatively and reflectively[3] – because we are not only individual but know that we are and because we are not only present to others but are present to ourselves – we find and make ourselves spontaneous beings that reach out in personal freedom, adaptation to others, and social order to challenge the logic of nothingness and chance. Moreover, in being thinking beings, we are able to ask questions about the nature of our being and the ground of being itself. Pascal again has said pithily: 'Man is only a reed, the most feeble thing in nature; but he is a thinking reed.'[4]

The question of origins that is raised over my/our personal existence hangs over all other existing things as well. Heidegger, the German thinker, argued that the 'ground question' in metaphysics is: 'Why is there any Being at all – why not far rather Nothing?'[5] It is not simply that every being presupposes other beings and so on *ad infinitum* (the Scholastics argued that this would involve an infinite regress unless there was a cause outside the series)[6] but the positive being of anything – the fact of existence in the case of any existent – challenges the logic of nothingness and the non-necessary nature of being as we meet it in ephemeral experience. We, humans, differ from other beings in being conscious of the question of existence and non-existence that is posed about them as it is posed about us. In other words, logically there need not be anything but there is something. Consequentially, if there is being – and since there is – we are driven intellectually to find an explanation for it. Moreover, if there is something now there must always have been something because from nothing nothing comes: *ex nihilo nihil*. Moving on from this position I want to integrate our understanding of the existence of God with a discussion of his nature – in other words, linking *that* God is with *what* he is.[7]

That something that has always existed is what we call God. Once we accept the existence of God, there is however no profounder mystery than that he has always existed: he is existence that is its own explanation; existence that must in some strange way explain all existence, including our ability to grow and to feel, to know and to love; existence that does not change and that yet possesses the fullness of freedom; existence that is unlimited and yet is something with which our limited being is able to co-exist.[8]

The central paradox of creation that underlies lesser issues such as those of divine foreknowledge and human freedom is that other beings can in some derived and limited way exist within – and exist in some way other than – infinite and unlimited being. Mother Julian of Norwich, the medieval anchorite, sketches a powerful image:

> He showed me a little thing, the size of a hazelnut, lying in the palm of my hand, and it was as round as a ball. I looked at it with my mind's eye and I thought, 'What can this be?' And answer came, 'It is all that is made.' I marvelled that it could last, for I thought it might have crumbled to nothing, it was so small. And the answer came into my mind. 'It lasts and ever shall because God loves it.'[9]

This paradox of creation involves, further, that the being of the creator is beyond or *transcendent* to the creature but the creator simultaneously pervades the being of the creature, or is *immanent* in it. God is outside and God is within. A prayer from a *Book of Hours* (1514) that is reproduced in *The Book of*

Common Prayer conveys the immanence of God while implying his transcendence:

> God be in my head and in my understanding;
> God be in my eyes and in my looking;
> God be in my mouth and in my speaking;
> God be in my heart and in my thinking;
> God be at my end and at my departing.

In short, in some strange way we are permeated by God because there is no being outside him; and we are other than God because we are finite and individual. So too, we are not persons in action over against God nor God over against us but in an almighty and mysterious way God respects our individuality while empowering our being.

THE PERSON OF GOD

Since we can think only by means of human concepts drawn from our experience of finite things, we have to think about God in ideas that are proper to us, not least in terms of personality. In other words, a certain anthropomorphism is inevitable in our thinking about God. Unfortunately God has been so crassly described down through the centuries – one has only to think of the elderly greybeard of many artists – that there have been inevitable reactions. Voltaire is reputed to have quipped: God is said to have made man to his image, we have returned him the favour. Yet God has to be understood as a person. For one thing, personality – like life, truth and freedom – involves no sense of inherent limitation. For another, personality is the finest flowering of the finite world and we cannot think of the First Cause as lacking in itself what it is responsible for in other beings. In the context of its Jewish inheritance, Christianity, by insisting on the personal nature of God – with Islam following this thinking – has reinforced an analytic and purified understanding of the ground of being that many other religions have had to struggle towards with difficulty.

In other words, in the source of being there must be subsisting life, knowledge and love – those elements that make up personality – since it is inconceivable that the source of being can be without attributes that crown being. Yet if knowledge and love are to be found in God, they must be his in an infinitely enhanced way and without the limits and defects of those features of life in the finite world. Also, since these attributes are infinite and identical with him, we can judge that they belong to God but we can no more think of them or expand upon adequate concepts of them as they exist in him than we can enclose him fully in our thinking. For that reason human generations have sought all through history to understand God better. In this process they are aware that infinite life and truth, while remaining outside full understanding, reveal themselves most clearly to those who unceasingly seek; and they reveal themselves differently in differing historical experiences. Finally, given the nature of God – the latter is spiritual because anything that is material is limited and divisible – it is obvious that he/she does not have the limitations of sexual being. Patriarchal traditions have thought of God in masculine terms. God however needs to be understood beyond the division of the sexes.[10]

FINDING THE FACE OF GOD

Given the nature of God and existence, it follows that we come to know God most surely through other people. We can come, in fact, to understand infinite truth and love only through experiencing truthful and loving persons as we can understand the forgiveness of God only through ourselves forgiving and being forgiven as well as observing the forgiveness of others. Even various sacred scriptures, and especially the Christian gospels, that suggest what we might look for in searching for God remain incapable of being understood without lived encounters with other persons: the scriptures are dead without those around us. Hence, to discern God we have to see him through facets of our experience: through the way, for example, a mother cuddles her child, through the courage with which an activist stands up for a persecuted minority, through the reverence for truth in the work of a committed scholar, through the healing power of love that is freely given by a beloved whom we love and respect. Hubert Halbfass puts this point well:

> To talk about God you do not have to use theological terms. The word 'God' itself is often unnecessary, and (as so often used) awakens the suspicion that what is being talked about is really a very, very long way away. Talking about one's wife, learning to live with an illness, saying what work really means to one; sharing one's love for a painting, or a poem: all this can be talk of God. It is not the 'what' that gives human language this 'content', but 'how'. Some people just speak about children, their house and garden, supper and bed, and yet their discourse is full of faith and hope, thanks and prayer.[11]

In short, if persons are the image of God, we are able to discern in them and through them and with them the features of God's face and experience the love of God's person. There is a rabbinical reply that is matched by a sentence from a philosopher. In a story a child asks a rabbi: 'Rabbi, Rabbi, why are people all so different?' The rabbi replied: 'Because they are all in the image of God.'[12] The philosopher, Émile Boutroux, said: 'The only way for the finite to imitate the infinite is to diversify itself infinitely.'[13]

In turn, in being our best selves we reveal to others the face of God. We are most like God – in a way non-human creatures are not – in sharing the creativity of his knowledge, love and freedom. We share divine creativity in our inventive endeavours to explain and organise reality, in our ample, if struggling, ability to love all that exists, and in our marvellous freedom to work out a commitment to others and to the Other.[14]

In dealing with God – as in dealing with other persons – love is central. Love itself is a mixture of reverence for the individuality of the other, a will to give, and a hope to receive. In reciprocated love the circle of love is completed: there is a spontaneous recognition between two persons and a reaching out that occurs at some moment in the development of love and continues on in the enduring giving of love. To repeat what has been said earlier: not only is there a first creative moment in love but such moments mark all its stages; and lovers, young and old, constantly see one another, reach out to one another, and give to one another, for the first time, just as the true mystic in turning to God in the most ritualised prayer forever recites the words for the first time. God is love;[15] and his greatest gift is to enable us to turn to him in the freshness of our love for him and for others. In a profound sense we learn about him from others; we reveal him to others; and we move towards him not only directly but through loving others.

So far I have discussed our knowing God, dominantly though not exclusively, from an intellectual viewpoint. It might be said that this approach is more knowing about God than knowing God, more about understanding God than experiencing him. Part of the difficulty in making this distinction is that our will follows on knowledge but in the case of God our knowledge inevitably falls short of him. We can however turn to God directly through our will. One of the most thoughtful of the theistic phenomenologists, Duméry, has written:

> ... the idea that we have of God is inevitably
> below God; its role is functional ... it is only
> the conceptual expression of the movement
> towards God; therefore, it remains human,
> limited, ambiguous, indefinitely purifiable,
> even when the movement of the soul which it
> takes into account is based on the absolute
> need that urges man to call himself totally into
> question (essence and existence) and to move
> beyond himself in all that he has, in all that he
> is.[16]

EXPERIENCING GOD

The question still remains: do we know or
encounter or experience God directly? It seems to
me that in three particular ways we do. First, we
meet God in the spontaneity of intellectual and
loving minds as well as in other spontaneities of
growth in the world. The poet, Patrick Kavanagh,
expresses something of this sense of God in the
experience of an Irish peasant, gaunt and hardened:

> He lives that his little fields may stay fertile when
> his own body
> Is spread in the bottom of a ditch under two coulters
> crossed in Christ's name (...)
> Yet sometimes when the sun comes through a gap
> These men knew God the Father in a tree:

The Holy Spirit in the rising sap,
And Christ will be the green leaves that will come
At Easter from the sealed and guarded tomb.[17]

Alongside finding God in the spontaneities of growth, those with eyes and ears to discern have recognised his infinity in the vast canopy of the starry sky, his eternity in the waves that sweep in from the ocean, his beauty in the multitudinous colours of the flowers, his voice in the music of the birds, and his silence in the gentle breeze.

Second, since we know that God recognises us and cares for us, we encounter him in the way that we experience someone who is looking at us – and we know that he is doing that. In this understanding we look back at God; we talk to him, and we know that he hears us and we know that, no matter how mysteriously, he in turn talks and takes the initiative, often with humour, in talking to us. There is also an element in the experience that resembles, though it does not quite duplicate, the way in which we encounter an author through his or her works. Third, we know God directly in experiencing existence: in meeting existence we encounter in some strange way its wholeness; we meet the whole in the part; and in experiencing finiteness we experience obscurely but profoundly the infinity that gives it existence.[18] Blake put this last insight into great and simple language:

> To see a World in a Grain of Sand,
>> And a Heaven in a Wild Flower,
> Hold Infinity in the palm of your hand,
>> And Eternity in an hour.[19]

I prefer to leave the more developed formulations of experiencing God to the mystics who have encountered him in an enhanced way and some of whom have put their experience into lucid words.[20] All I am contending here is that I think there is direct experience of God. Moreover, this direct experience is lit up by the intellectual discernment that I have earlier written about, just as it is nourished by the encounter of persons.

Finally, in direct experience between persons – in the reciprocity of awarenesses – there are two subjects: if we experience God, God communicates himself to us beyond the subject-object duality which his infinity transcends. Hence, we are not persons over against God nor God over against us but in an almighty and mysterious manner God leaves our individuality intact while transfusing our very being.

In understanding our relations with God in an inter-personal way and in integrating our relations with God into the exigencies of human love, the Christian tradition – like other theistic traditions – has emphasised that in the hearts of humans there is a longing for God, for the infinite, for what holds out to us hope of eventually solving problems of truth, righting issues of injustice, and fulfilling the desires of love: 'You have made us for yourself, O God,' said Augustine, 'and our hearts are restless, ever restless, until they rest in you.'[21] In other words, nothing limited satisfies us fully and whatever we reach invites us to move further; and so within us there is a sign of a relentless dynamism that prompts us to move beyond every achievement.

Though Augustine's exclamation may have been prompted by Christianity, it does not depend on the latter. Indeed all Christianity does in this respect is to suggest that our eventual move towards the infinite will lead to greater intimacy than reason left to itself would have suspected or guessed at. Moreover, reflections on our origins and on the human coherence of a world in which we both find and give meanings integrate rational logic and ethical goodness into our understanding of our relations with God, that is, with the Other, as well as with all the others. With such intellectual and moral conclusions a theist avoids the logic of irrationality and the ethics of despair that enter into Sartre's declaration: '… l'homme est une passion inutile' ('… man is a useless passion').[22]

Though we may long for unity with the infinite, what we – finite, flawed and sinful beings – cannot do is to merit the infinite God. Moreover, if God is love – and if God has first loved us – love, whether divine or human love, cannot be merited but has to be freely given. Yet love has also to be freely responded to. So humans possess a fearful prerogative: they can reject the offer of God's love. To reject God definitively is what hell is. God who made us without our consent, said Augustine, cannot take us to himself without our consent.[23] The possibility of hell is the inevitable concomitant of human freedom.

If hell is the willed absence of God, heaven is the company of God. Indeed since we do not go alone to God, heaven is also the company of others whom we love in God. A generation ago Sartre wrote that hell was other people: '… l'Enfer, c'est les autres' (*Huis Clos*). The truth is, however, that heaven is other people who love, and the Other, who is love. With more insight, another French novelist and thinker, Georges Bernanos, has written: 'Hell … is to love no more.'[24] Yet while we must retain the human right to reject God and to hold open the possibility of hell, I personally believe that a God of power and goodness will in some way be able to make all of us offers that we cannot refuse.[25]

LOVE, PURIFICATION AND REFLECTION

Just as Goethe said that we had to work for the gifts that our ancestors handed on to us, so do we have to work for the gift of God's love. Indeed we have to work for human love too since persons, in loving one another, go through profoundly purifying experiences as they adapt to one another and grow in intimacy with one another. Since we grow through process, we cannot relate to God 'once-and-for-all' but in our best selves and all through our lives, during which we work on a love match with him. Moreover, we flawed and sinful creatures need to be powerfully purified in going to God and made painfully, if gloriously and lovingly, ready for full intimacy with this God of holiness, truth and love.[26] The medievals attempted to formulate this truth in the doctrine of purgatory – Dante in his *Purgatorio* gave it marvellous expression. Purgatory is simply a way of conceiving the purification of those who are impure on their way to the all-holy intimacy of infinite love. We have no idea of the time or process of such purification but know that it must happen for the finite to reach the infinite in a way that enables the finite to receive in a personal way the gift of infinite love. Hopkins evokes the struggle of human love coming purifyingly to terms with divine love:

Me? or me that fought him? O which one? is it
each one?
That night, that year
Of now done darkness I wretch lay wrestling
with (my God!)
My God.[27]

It is however in this struggle with the God of love
that we grow in love and freedom and beauty.

Moreover, at the heart of this struggle lies
reconciliation. Historically, humankind – and each
individual human – needs to return to God in the
wake of sin, which is a break with God and with
others. God takes the initiative in forgiveness,
coming as it does out of love, but it is an initiative
that we in our turn are called to join.

In God we live and move and have our being.
But to recognise the fundamental context and
conditions of our existence we need to make space
for God. It is here that the principle of the sabbath
comes into operation. Through the sabbath we stand
back from our workaday lives; we organise time that
we give to God, to others and to ourselves. In our
contemporary circumstances we may not have to
locate the sabbath in one day each week, but we
have to structure our lives to provide us with
occasions for worship, thought and silence as well as
for family and social intercourse. To put these ideas

in another way: if we are always to pray, there must be moments that are nothing but prayer; if we are always to love, there must be actions that are nothing but love; and if we are to be always with God, there must be moments when we are with him only.

Prayer and reflection are crucial to giving a proper worth to reality. While some things force their presence on us, there are many worthwhile things that we won't heed unless we are already prepared to look for them. Wordsworth wrote about a particular heap of stones that 'you might pass by, / Might see and notice not'.[28] We see lots of things that we don't notice; and if things have to be drawn to our notice, then it often happens that we still don't properly see them because the prompt comes from outside and is not inner initiated or taken hold of. We live with the great paradox that we find God in searching for him and only search for him having already in some measure found him. Pascal expresses this conviction in saying: 'You would not seek me had you not already found me.'[29]

THE PARADOX OF SILENCE AND RESPONSE

Yet given the infinite and eternal nature of God, we are faced with enormous problems of relating to him. In many respects the simple relationship with

God is love. But we who are transitory, threatened and guilty seek his help in dealing with insecurity, coping with illness and the menace of death, and wanting forgiveness for wrong-doing.[30] Moreover, we have come from generations of peasant ancestors who time and again in their need sought the direct help of God. But now in a technological and urban age we have created new powers of control, communication and comfort that appear to diminish the need for the erstwhile intermittent interventions of God and that reduce – or even eliminate – the role of God in our lives. We have also sought to distance ourselves from a sense of sin and have tried to remove the notion of human fault from its religious roots. For such reasons Nietzsche could mock: God is dead. The God of the gaps – as indeed the divine Custodian of clerical morality – is indeed dead but he is not our God. Our God is not the God who is present when one pilgrim plane lands safely and who is absent when the other pilgrim plane crashes. Our God is not the upholder of established order. We may be impelled psychologically to think of God as the occasional listener to troubled prayers or as the shadow darkening our conscience; and we may be tempted to perceive him as the spasmodic intervener in our affairs or as the alien judge of our actions. But those images are no more adequate than those of the elderly greybeard.

The truth is that we have to live with simultaneous austerity and abundance in the presence of God; we have to live with his felt absence and with his overwhelming presence; we owe our being totally to him, yet we are co-creators with him in the world about us; we have to rely on his help and know that it is never denied us while yet being unable to recognise its presence;[31] we are closer to him than we are to ourselves but we have to live in the search for him; we are meant all the time to talk to him with familiarity and affection, while knowing that he is beyond all that we are; we may stray from him from time to time but he seeks our return unceasingly; we are utterly answerable to him and we are entirely responsible to ourselves; we work only through the powers that he gives us, and yet the achievement remains entirely ours. In short, God is everywhere; and he is nowhere. God does everything; and he does nothing. God hears our prayers; and he never intervenes. God achieves his will; and we are free.

GOD, ETERNITY AND TIME

The metaphysical reflections of the previous paragraph – and of this chapter generally – are meant only to underpin our living relationship with God. In that relationship we cannot talk about him from memory because he is not in the past; and we cannot think about him as absent because he is not even as far away as the next room. We live in his presence and his love in the way that we live in the warmth of a human love reciprocated. We cannot always be thinking about him but even without turning our minds directly to him, we remain all the time mindful of him in the way that a happily married man or woman is aware of the presence of their partner and their children during the most engrossing work or during a period away from them. We possess him in waiting for him. Our glance moves to him from time to time and meets his glance. We walk with him along the way; and he waits for us at the end.

In a final thought, we might linger on the manner in which we live between time and eternity. Eternity is God: the simultaneous and total possession of endless life (Boethius).[32] It seems worth noticing here that heaven/God's company/eternity must escape our conceptualisation as God does. Emil Brunner reminds us:

> Eternal life is not an unending continuance of this life – that would perhaps be Hell – but eternal life is a quite different life, divine, not

mundane, perfect, not earthly, true life, not corrupt half-life.[33]

Within and alongside and towards that eternity our time moves. In consequence, we have to live with a paradox: we are meant never to hold on to the fleeting moment; and we have to hold on entirely to that moment which is all we possess; we have to accept that all that we do is transitory; and yet we need to appreciate each moment for its own worth, deal with it in its own right, and treasure it exclusive of all other moments. In a sense the challenge for us is to cherish time without clinging to it or being carried away by it. It is, finally, in accepting simultaneously our finitude and our reach for the infinite that we take hold of time and work with God to turn time into eternity.

NOTES

1   To say that I am contingent is to say that I exist but need not have done so. Contingency enters into the distinction between creaturehood and finitude. Through the concept of creaturehood, persons recognise existential limitations in accepting a theistic view of creation; and through finitude, persons recognise limitations without necessarily involving a theistic reference. While creaturehood is rejected in much modern philosophy, the most explicit rejection of finiteness by the assertion of complete human moral autonomy is to be found in Sartre's work. To illustrate the distinction between creaturehood and finitude, one might go to literature and mention three considerable novels that deal with creaturehood: Fyodor Dostoyevsky, *The Idiot*; Nathaniel Hawthorne, *The Scarlet Letter*; and Graham Greene, *The Power and the Glory*; and three considerable novels that deal with finiteness: Emily Bronte, *Wuthering Heights*; Henry James, *The Golden Bowl*; and D.H. Lawrence, *The Rainbow*.

2 *Pensées*, 205, 206 (Collection Internationale), New York, 1961.

3 In a special issue of the *Scientific American* entitled 'Mind and Brain', which was heavily oriented towards the biological foundations of consciousness, memory and other attributes of mind, Jonathan Miller wrote a short paper, 'Trouble in Mind', that argues that the connection between mind and brain is ultimately irreducible. He quotes Einstein, who said that the most incomprehensible fact about nature was that it was comprehensible. Heidegger, let it be said, makes the same point in his study of Kant and points to the metaphysics implicit in Kant's recognition of the manner in which the mind is geared to understanding the universe. Miller goes on to say – beyond Einstein – that 'the mysterious thing about nature is not that it is comprehensible but that it contains such a thing as comprehension at all, that is, the mind itself – the very idea!' Further, he discusses the nature of introspection and points out that the latter is not an invisible property but that '... my consciousness, if I have it at all, is self-evidently self-evident to me.' (*Scientific American*, September, 1992, p. 132.) Built into these considerations is the spontaneity of the mind, the given (what the mind meets) that the mind recognises, and the meaning that the mind gives to the given in placing it within an order conditioned by the encounter of the spontaneity of the mind, acquired categories and external existents. Finally, a metaphysical question on ultimate explanation arises out of the order between the different elements of reality and in particular out of the relationship between the comprehension of the mind and the reality internal and external to it.

4 *Pensées*, 347, op. cit.

5 *Existence and Being* (English trans.), Chicago, 1949, p. 349.

6 For that reason the Scholastics argued that the infinite was not the first link in a long chain but was other than any finite series.

7 I am conscious of the reproach made to Christianity by Leslie Dewart who argues that the latter religion is prone to the temptation which is '... the subordination of the meaning of God to the fact of his existence. Christianity enjoys the doubtful distinction of being the only higher religion to have become preoccupied with the existence of God to the extent of having neglected his reality.' *The Future of Belief: Theism in a World Come of Age*, New York, 1966, pp. 71–2.

8 Though empirical scientists raise questions concerning the existence and nature of God, they do not by and large take on the question of existence: why is there something rather than nothing? But many of them also do not raise a second question: how has it happened in a limited time and against extraordinarily statistical odds that intelligent life has come about in a

highly diverse and fine-tuned universe? They do however concern themselves at great length with a third question which their methods are suitable for answering: by what stages did intelligent life emerge?

9   *Revelations of Divine Love*, Chapter 5. The most accessible edition of Julian's work is the one by Backhouse and Pipe (Hodder and Stoughton), 1987.

10 Mother Julian grasped that God could not be understood without reference to motherhood as well as to fatherhood. She says: 'I say that God rejoices that he is our father, and God rejoices that he is our mother …' She also wrote that '… God is all natural goodness. He is the ground, he is the being, he is the essence of what is natural. He is the true Father and true Mother of all natural things …' *Revelations of Divine Love*, Chapter 62.

11 *Theory of Catechetics* (English trans.), New York, 1971, p. 136.

12 The story is retold in Marie Balmary, *Le sacrifice interdit*, Paris, 1986, p. 277.

13 *Sciences et religion dans la philosophie contemporaine*, Paris, 1947, p. 392.

14 Underlying the relationship of God and others that is described in the text is an understanding of persons as historical, social and growing. Hence, morality is, on the one hand, based on persons creating themselves freely, though not arbitrarily, in the context of their history and their societies and, on the other hand, dealing with contemporary problems that take in issues of peace and war, working for justice between countries and within countries, overcoming racial, class and gender divisions, and supporting freedom and human rights everywhere in the world. There is a profoundly individual dimension to our relationship with God, but a purely individual relationship with God would travesty the fellowship among us that relating to God brings with it. Moreover, we might keep in mind what Baron von Hügel wrote to Evelyn Underhill, the English mystic, about the structure of the most individual experience: 'The mystic sense flies straight to God and thinks it finds all its delights in Him alone. But a careful examination always discovers many sensible, institutional, and historical contributions to this supposed ineffable experience.' Cited in Anne Bancroft, *Weavers of Wisdom: Women Mystics of the Twentieth Century*, Penguin, 1989, p. 91.

15 There is Dante's oft-cited line: 'The love that moves the sun and the other stars.' ('*L'amor che muove il sole e l'altre stelle.*') *Paradiso*, Canto V.

16 *Le problème de Dieu*, Tournai, 1957, p. 78.

17 Patrick Kavanagh, 'The Great Hunger'.

18 Charles Peirce, the American founder of pragmatism, wrote that religion was in each individual '… a sort of sentiment, or obscure perception, a deep recognition of something in the circumambient All, which, if he tries to express it will clothe itself in forms more or less extravagant, more or less

accidental, but ever acknowledging the first and last, the Alpha and Omega, as well as a relation to that Absolute of the individual's self, as a relative being.' *Collected Works*, Cambridge, Mass., 1931–35, Vol. 6, par. 429.

19 'Auguries of Innocence'.

20 Two poems that immediately come to mind from Hopkins on the experience of God are 'As Kingfishers Catch Fire' and 'God's Grandeur'.

21 *Confessions*, Book I, Chapter 1.

22 *L'être et le néant*, Paris, 1943, p. 708.

23 *Sermon* 169.

24 *Journal d'un curé de campagne*, Paris, 1936.

25 Dante has a comment: 'The Infinite Goodness has such wide arms that it takes whatever turns to it.' *Purgatorio*, Canto III.

26 Kierkegaard remarked: 'Between man and truth lies mortification – you can see why we are all more or less afraid.' *Journals*. T.S. Eliot wrote: 'Human kind / Cannot bear very much reality.' 'Burnt Norton', pt. 1.

27 'Carrion Comfort'.

28 'Michael'.

29 *Pensées*, 553, op. cit, p. 148.

30 Dante suggests with felicitous insight: 'And in his will is our peace.' (*'E'n la sua voluntade é nostra pace.'*) *Paradiso*, Canto III.

31 It may be objected that this view contradicts the view that we experience God directly. Yet in social intercourse the fact that we relate to a person does not necessarily mean that we know what he or she immediately thinks or intends.

32 *De consolatione philosophiae*, III, par. 6.

33 *Our Faith* (English trans.), London, 1949, p. 121.

II

THE GOD OF ISRAEL:
FROM ABRAHAM
TO MARY

GOD OF ABRAHAM, GOD OF ISAAC, GOD OF JACOB,
NOT OF THE PHILOSOPHERS AND SCHOLARS ...

PASCAL

In dealing with the Hebrew concept of God I want
to focus mainly on how the Jews understood God
in the period immediately before Christ. It was that
understanding of God among his contemporaries
that Jesus took for granted in his teaching.

However, I want to start by calling attention to
changes that the scriptures reveal in Jewish thinking
about God. Such thinking evolved over long
periods of time as a small and beleaguered but
highly articulate people gradually came to
understand more accurately and profoundly the
source of their being and their nationhood. Yet
people of those centuries had little sense of
historical development – until modern historical
scholarship got under way in the nineteenth

century, the same was true in the Christian era. For such reasons people tended to see their scriptures or written religious sources as one document or book, which they quarried in the light of views prevailing in the community. Also, those who at a late stage in Jewish history put the biblical documents together reworked the material in them to make them more consistent with views held when they were compiled. It is also worth remarking that the Jews reached their understanding of the one God in the midst of polytheistic peoples who were in many instances much more militarily powerful and more cultured than themselves.

THE DEVELOPMENT OF THE IDEA OF GOD AMONG THE JEWS

The contrasting descriptions in the opening chapters of Genesis suggest already the different sources and experiences of God that led up to and lay behind the later Jewish beliefs. In the earliest documents of the Bible – scholars call them the J or Yahwist source because in them God is called Yahweh (Jahve) – God has strongly human characteristics (Genesis, chapters 1 and 2). To make Adam, he takes up clay from the ground, fashions it, and then breathes on it to render him a living spirit. God then makes Eve from a rib plucked from Adam. In a similarly homely vein, God walks in the garden of paradise. Yet flanking and preceding these accounts we find a philosophical account of the making of man and woman – this is from the P or priestly document; male and female he made them; and the making of the world was modelled on the seven-day organisation of worship in the temple. The P document was written centuries later than the material that the J document uses. But the compilers of Genesis thought there were riches in putting the two accounts of human-making side by side.[1]

Initially the Jews recognised that other peoples rightly had their gods who were powerful in their particular territories (Judges 9:24; 4 Kings 3:27). At an early stage of their own understanding of Yahweh, they simply argued that their God was stronger than the gods of their neighbours and looked after them better, not least in leading them to victory in battle and giving them the land that he had promised them. Indeed when David was faced with exile, he complained that he was being driven away to serve other gods and deprived of the Lord who was his heritage (1 Samuel 27:19). As the Jews gradually deepened their sense of God, they came however more strongly to understand that there was only one God. They refined this sense of God until by the time of the Deutero-Isaiah they understood that not only was there only one God but there could only be one God.[2] Isaiah writes about the uniqueness of God and his people's testimony to their Lord:

> You are my witnesses, says the Lord, and my servant whom I have chosen, so that you may know and believe me and understand that I am he. Before me no god was formed, nor shall there be any after me … I am the Lord, your Holy One, the Creator of Israel, your King.
> (Isa 43:10, 15)

Once the Jews came to believe that the other gods were illusory, they mocked that they had eyes but could not see, ears but could not hear, mouths but could not speak (Psalms 116). Yet many among them were time and again tempted to turn to the idols of the peoples around them, idols that offered a less austere and more visible access to the powers of the universe.[3] Their best leaders and prophets rejected such temptations and constantly called the people back from veneration of idols to faithfulness to Yahweh whose spiritual nature was such that he should not be represented (Deuteronomy 4:15).

In other words, the Jews were an earthy people, of limited culture, no more religious than many others, ever eager for proofs and tangible signs of divine help but also able to discover and preserve a particularly pure understanding of a transcendent being; they nourished in their midst personalities of exceptional ability, especially the prophets, who time and again called them back to the primacy of divine love-giving, the worth of collective faithfulness to God and his law, and, not least, a sense of individual responsibility.

They struggled to find images to describe this God, the Holy One of Israel (2 Kings 19:22): they likened him to a king, shepherd, father, mother, husband or potter; and they called him a lion and a rock. At the heart of Jewish thinking about God in every period of their history lies their understanding of him as a person; and much of their religious and literary effort is to build up a portrait of him as a person. If their initial experience of God is collective – and there are the great dual interacting symbols of God and his people: God-Father, Israel-son; God-fiancé, Israel-fiancée; God-husband, Israel-wife; God-Master, Israel-servant – then with time the relationship, while remaining an alliance with the whole people, becomes also more individual and personal. In strong yet gentle language, Hosea develops one of these images in a depiction of God's relations with his people:

> And I will take you for my wife forever; I will take you for my wife in righteousness and in

> justice, in steadfast love, and in mercy. I will
> take you for my wife in faithfulness; and you
> shall know the Lord. (Hos 2:19-20)

If we want a superb expression of where the Jews
had eventually arrived at in their understanding of
God, we cannot do better than to turn to verses put
in the mouth of Mary in the Magnificat (or for that
matter to the Benedictus of Zechariah or the Nunc
dimittis of Simeon), which is full of phrases from
the Hebrew scriptures, especially from the song of
Hannah (1 Samuel 2:1-10) and the psalms. The
idealised sentiments in the verses of the song of
Mary belong not only to the mother of Jesus but to
the Jewish people of God:

> And Mary said,
> My soul magnifies the Lord,
> and my spirit rejoices in God my Saviour,
> For he has looked with favour
> on the lowliness of his servant.
> Surely, from now on all generations
> will call me blessed;
> for the Mighty One has done
> great things for me,
> and holy is his name.
> His mercy is for those who fear him
> from generation to generation.
> He has shown strength with his arm;

he has scattered the proud in
the thoughts of their hearts.
He has brought down
the powerful from their thrones,
and lifted up the lowly;
he has filled the hungry with good things,
and sent the rich away empty.
He has helped his servant Israel,
in remembrance of his mercy,
according to the promise he
made to our ancestors,
to Abraham and to his
descendants forever. (Lk 1:46-55)

THE HOLY ONE OF ISRAEL

The power of God and his distance from humans
were expressed by the Jews in the attribute that is
time and again given to God: holy.[4] At one and the
same time it describes a feature of life that is proper
to God, that separates him from flawed humans, and
yet that in measure God expects of human persons.
Isaiah emphasises the difference:

> To whom then will you compare me, or who is
> my equal? says the Holy One. (Isa 40:25)

One may notice that the Magnificat refers to God's
name being holy, and Jesus takes this theme up in the
prayer that he taught his disciples. Yet while there are

not many references in the Christian scriptures to God's holiness, it is a recurring and salient characteristic of God in the Hebrew scriptures. The psalms urge:

> Extol the Lord our God; worship at his footstool. Holy is he! (Ps 99:5)

The living God is the holy one, the holy one of Israel. There is a mysterious otherness of God: he belongs to a realm of power beyond humans; he is pure; and he can be approached only by the pure. Isaiah was called to his mission through a vision that brings together these divine features:

> … I saw the Lord sitting on a throne, high and lofty; and the hem of his robe filled the temple. Seraphs were in attendance above him … they covered their faces … And one called to the other and said:
>
> > 'Holy, holy, holy is the Lord of hosts;
> > the whole earth is full of his glory.' …
>
> And I said: 'Woe is me! I am lost, for I am a man of unclean lips, and I live among people of unclean lips; yet my eyes have seen the King, the Lord of hosts!' Then one of the seraphs flew to me, holding a live coal that had been taken from the altar with a pair of tongs. The seraph touched my mouth with it and said: 'Now that this has touched your lips, your guilt has departed and your sin is blotted out.' (Isa 6:1-7)

Then, purified and commissioned, Isaiah volunteers to go to his people.

More often than anyone else, Isaiah refers to the 'Holy One of Israel'.[5] But already Amos and Hosea had emphasised this holiness, which evokes the sense of separateness and remoteness of God and his being wholly other. Amos stresses that to be holy is the proper nature of God (Amos 4:2); and Hosea has Yahweh swear by his holiness (Hosea 41:2). Earlier than the superb concepts of God in the Isaiahan documents, Hosea, one of the first writing prophets, has God say:

> ... for I am God and no mortal, the Holy One in your midst, and I will not come in wrath. (Hos 11:9)

In Exodus, God is addressed:

> Who is like you, O Lord, among the gods?
> Who is like you, majestic in holiness, awesome in splendour, doing wonders. (Ex 15:11)

What the great prophets – Isaiah, Jeremiah and Ezekiel – did was to deepen this sense of holiness which humans catch sight of with fear and trembling and which abhors sin and exercises power over the forces of evil. These prophets describe the power that reaches out to all things and the integrity that touches lives. In short, God is fearful but fascinating. Isaiah had good reason to be afraid and yet be drawn to his mission.

Since God is holy and shows this holiness through his searing life and his righteous judgements of love and justice, his people are – and have to be – holy too: 'For I am the Lord your God; sanctify yourselves therefore, and be holy, for I am holy' (Lev 11:44). This holiness comes about through their faith in the one God, their liturgical worship, their following of rules that make them a distinctive people, and their lives of goodness and justice in observing the commandments. Through these means the Jewish people are enabled to cope with the holiness of God – his power, purity and distance – and they are in some measure able to bridge the chasm between the holy power of God and their own limited and flawed holiness. In terms of priorities however, faithfulness to God in righteousness is essential; and so ritual is subordinate to justice and mercy. Psalm 50 castigates those who offer sacrifice but who do not observe justice and fidelity; and it goes on to deepen the concept of sacrifice:

> Those who bring thanksgiving as their sacrifice honour me; to those who go the right way I will show the salvation of God. (Ps 50:23)

Elsewhere a psalmist writes lines of thanksgiving and petition:

> Sacrifice and offering you do not desire, but you have given me an open ear. Burnt offering and sin offering you have not required. Then I said, 'Here I am; in the scroll of the book it is written of me. I delight to do your will, O my God; your law is within my heart.' (Ps 40:6-8)

Holiness is deeply linked to justice: Amos, Isaiah, Jeremiah and Ezekiel lay great stress on the justice of God, his concern for the weak and the poor, and his rejection of those who trample on the poor (Amos 2:7). For Isaiah:

> … if you offer your food to the hungry and satisfy the needs of the afflicted, then your light shall rise in the darkness and your gloom be like the noonday. (Isa 58:10)

In a word, the holiness of the people comes from their entry into the presence of God and from their upright relations with one another, especially when the relations of the powerful and the rich with the weak and the poor are just and compassionate.

YAHWEH: THE GOD OF POWER AND HOLINESS WHO IS ALSO NEAR

In their developed concept of God, the Jews had a sense of his overwhelming power and enduring being. Isaiah describes him:

THE MYSTERY OF BEING: THE PRESENCE AND ABSENCE OF GOD

> ... I am the Lord, and there is no other. I form
> light and create darkness, I make weal and create
> woe; I the Lord do all these things. (Isa 45:6-7)

The essence of Jewish monotheistic faith is
expressed in central passages of Deuteronomy:[6]

> ... The Lord is our God, the Lord alone. You
> shall love the Lord your God with all your
> heart, and with all your soul, and with all your
> might ... For what other great nation has a god
> so near to it as the Lord our God is whenever
> we call to him? And what other great nation
> has statutes and ordinances as just as this entire
> law that I am setting before you today?
> (Deut 6:4-5; 4:7-8)

In other words, if God is transcendent, he is also
near. One of the principal ways in which the
nearness of God is expressed is through the idea and
role of God as father, which Jesus will take up so
fully.[7] In the frequent use of this image (as well as
related images), the holiness of God, which can be
so daunting, recedes into the background so that
the nearness of God and the care of God can be
communicated. If God, then, is father, Israel has the
rights of a son. Moses is told: 'Then you shall say to
Pharaoh, "Thus says the Lord: Israel is my first-born
son"' (Ex 4:22). Hosea writes tenderly: 'When Israel

was a child, I loved him, and out of Egypt I called my son' (Hos 11:1). More graphically again, Hosea writes about a father and his young child:

> Yet it was I who taught Ephraim to walk, I took them up in my arms; but they did not know that I healed them. I led them with cords of human kindness, with bands of love. I was to them like those who lift infants to their cheeks. I bent down to them and fed them. (Hos 11:3-4)

In a rare use of maternal images, Isaiah employs a powerful analogy to convey God's love:

> Can a woman forget her nursing child, or show no compassion for the child of her womb? Even these may forget, yet I will not forget you. (Isa 49:15)

What sustained the Jews during many difficult years is that they believed that this God had established a covenant or alliance with them, initially with Abraham as they began as a people, and later Moses as they were restored as a people after their stay in Egypt. Behind this belief is the understanding that God himself has taken the initiative in searching for his people, in choosing them, and in offering them the means through which they can be holy. Moses is described as celebrating the alliance in a mysterious communal meal:

> For you are a people holy to the Lord your God; the Lord your God has chosen you out of all the peoples on earth to be his people, his treasured possession. (Deut 7:6)

Ezekiel tells how God in his love took the initiative:
> I passed by you … and looked on you; you were at the age for love. I spread the edge of my cloak over you, and covered your nakedness: I pledged myself to you and entered into a covenant with you, says the Lord God, and you became mine. (Ezek 16:8)

In Exodus, God makes a precious promise:
> … if you obey my voice and keep my covenant, you shall be my treasured possession out of all the peoples. Indeed, the whole earth is mine, but you shall be for me a priestly kingdom and a holy nation. (Ex 19:5-6)

Jeremiah in pithy words outlines the covenant:
> For in the day that I brought your ancestors out of the land of Egypt … this command I gave them, 'Obey my voice, and I will be your God, and you shall be my people …' (Jer 7:22-23)

The covenant or alliance was at one and the same time the guarantee of God's love for Israel, the path that he wanted them to follow, and the measure by which the people were judged when they failed in fidelity. Over time its nature changed and the prophets were the heralds of that change.

Yet though the descriptions of the prophets overflow with God's love for his people, this God of mercy was also a God of justice, and he threatened those who betrayed the trust that he reposed in them. Through Isaiah he addressed the notables of the people:

> Ah, you who make iniquitous decrees, who write oppressive statutes, to turn aside the needy from justice and to rob the poor of my people of their right, that widows may be your spoil, and that you may make the orphans your prey! What will you do on the day of punishment, in the calamity that will come from far away? To whom will you flee for help, and where will you leave your wealth …?
> (Isa 10:1-3)

A NEW COVENANT

The Jews struggled with the problems of living with God. For long they accepted a doctrine of collective responsibility both in rewards and in punishment. They saw God punishing the nation with a famine for David's pride in holding a census; and they believed that God visited the results of sin on subsequent generations – Exodus speaks of God 'punishing children for the iniquity of parents, to the third and the fourth generation …' (Ex 20:5). The Jews were forced however with time to acknowledge that the good did not always prosper and that the wicked went unpunished. This acknowledgement as well as a growth in awareness of individual responsibility came into being and developed with a sensitising of consciences. In a superb dialogue, Jeremiah sets aside the facile belief that the faithful enjoy success and prosperity. Yet he feels the unfairness of the misfortunes of the just, and he remonstrates with God as Job would also do:

> You will be in the right, O Lord, when I lay charges against you; but let me put my case to you. Why does the way of the guilty prosper? Why do all who are treacherous thrive? You plant them, and they take root; they grow and bring forth fruit; you are near in their mouths yet far from their hearts. But you, O Lord, know me; You see me and test me – my heart is with you. (Jer 12:1-3)[8]

Ezekiel in rejecting collective guilt says:

> The person who sins shall die. A child shall not suffer for the iniquity of a parent, nor a parent suffer for the iniquity of a child; the righteousness of the righteous shall be his own,

and the wickedness of the wicked shall be his own. (Ezek 18:20)

Jeremiah had earlier warned individuals trenchantly:
> … Turn now, every one of you from your evil way and wicked doings … (Jer 25:5)

While the observances of ritual laws remained strong and helped to keep a distinctive national consciousness in being, the prophets more and more stressed forms of integrity that reached into every part of social and individual life and made not only the people but the individual holy. With Jeremiah and Ezekiel, the understanding of upright conduct is put into a new approach by God to his people, which evokes this more personalised response to him:

> The days are surely coming, says the Lord, when I will make a new covenant with the house of Israel and the house of Judah. It will not be like the covenant that I made with their ancestors when I took them by the hand to bring them out of the land of Egypt – a covenant they broke, though I was their husband, says the Lord. But this is the covenant that I will make with the house of Israel after those days, says the Lord: I will put my law within them and I will write it on their hearts;

and I will be their God, and they shall be my
people. (Jer 31:31-33)

Ezekiel continues the sense of inner renewal:

A new heart I will give you, and a new spirit I
will put within you; and I will remove from
your body the heart of stone and give you a
heart of flesh. (Ezek 36:26)

Behind the spiritualisation of the covenant lay
military defeat and the deportation of many Jews to
Babylon. The captivity in Babylon broke the Jews as
an organised nation. They retained the sense of being
a people but they knew how vulnerable they were to
outsiders and realised that they had to organise as
local communities of worship ('the assembly of
God') that would continue their traditions, maintain
the covenant with God, and look forward to the
fulfilment of the divine promises.

Since the changes in their circumstances brought
with them within the community an enhanced
sense of the relationship of the individual with God,
personal piety grew in quality. There is the longing
that a great-souled Augustine would centuries later
express: 'You have made us for yourself, O God and
our hearts are restless, ever restless, until they rest in
you.'[9] The Psalmist is more graphic:

> As a deer longs for flowing streams, so my soul longs for you, O God. My soul thirsts for God, for the living God. (Ps 42:1-2)

There is, particularly in the later psalms, a growth of dialogue with God that many centuries later still nourishes our own personal piety. One of the greatest of the psalms embodies the new outlook:

> Create in me a clean heart, O God, and put a new and right spirit within me. Do not cast me away from your presence, and do not take your holy spirit from me. Restore to me the joy of your salvation, and sustain in me a willing spirit. … The sacrifice acceptable to God is a broken spirit; a broken and contrite heart, O God, you will not despise. (Ps 51:10-12, 17)

Another psalm again expresses this sense of personal relationship with God:

> In you, O Lord, I seek refuge; do not let me ever be put to shame; in your righteousness deliver me. … Be a rock of refuge for me, a strong fortress to save me. You are indeed my rock and my fortress; for your name's sake lead me and guide me, take me out of the net that is hidden for me, for your are my refuge. Into your hand I commit my spirit; you have redeemed me, O Lord, faithful God. (Ps 31:1-5)

Longing for God, concern for others and the acceptance of his will come together in the strength of the tradition. When the old Jew, Simeon, takes the child Jesus into his arms, he thanks God and accepts for himself a death that is not far off. He goes on to tell the mother of the child that the latter is destined to be opposed and that a sword will pierce her own soul (Lk 2:29-35). He lives in a culmination of the faith of Isaiah, Jeremiah and Ezekiel.

Alongside the deepening of the individual's relationship with God, there was also among the prophets and psalmists and other faithful witnesses a spiritualising of the understanding of community that would provide a way for the coming together of Jews and Gentiles. Here we find a vision of a glorious ending of history in which God reigns and humankind lives unblemished. Simeon too sees in the destinies of Jesus and Mary a Jewish outreach to the Gentiles: ' … a light for revelation to the Gentiles and for glory to your people Israel' (Lk 2:32).

THE END OF THE EXILE AND THE CALLING OF THE NATIONS

The power, faithfulness and concern of God, which underlay his relationship with the Jewish people collectively and had progressed into the personal relationship of each individual with him, took on an original perspective as the Jews faced up to their new and exposed, but also more extended, relations with the peoples around them during the exile and afterwards. If they realised that Yahweh was the God of all the nations, and if they were grateful to Cyrus, the Persian ruler, for setting them free from Babylon, they could not ignore God's relations with peoples other than themselves. A Greek Jew, possibly from Alexandria, expresses the understanding that lay behind moves towards universalism:

> … the spirit of the Lord has filled the world … For your immortal spirit is in all things. … For neither is there any god beside you, whose care is for all the people … (Wis 1:7; 12:1, 13)

The new approach takes on shape in two related developments. First, the Jews will return from exile to Palestine and Jerusalem. Second, the nations will come to Jerusalem to worship Yahweh.

Jeremiah initially announces that God will bring back his people from captivity among the nations and establish with them an everlasting covenant. In his declarations he uses a new language that draws on the living worship of hearts:

> See, I am going to gather them from all the lands to which I drove them in my anger and my wrath and in great indignation; I will bring

> them back to this place, and I will settle them
> in safety. They shall be my people, and I will be
> their God. I will give them one heart and one
> way, that they may fear me for all time, for their
> own good and the good of their children after
> them. I will make an everlasting covenant with
> them, never to draw back from doing good to
> them; and I will put the fear of me in their
> hearts, so that they may not turn from me.
> (Jer 32:37-40)

Then, as the trappings of Jewish nationhood were
broken, a more purified sense of God was
elaborated, personal piety grew, and relations with
other peoples were forced into new contours.
Those faithful and thoughtful witnesses, the
prophets realised that the God of Israel, who was
the one and only God of the universe, cared for all
peoples and that the community originally
promised to the Jews could be extended to other
peoples. In a statement that anticipates the reply of
Jesus to the Samaritan woman about where God
would be worshipped, Jeremiah sets aside a long
tradition that had linked Yahweh to Sinai, various
centres of worship in Palestine, and the Ark and the
Temple:

> … in those days, says the Lord, they shall no
> longer say, 'The ark of the covenant of the

Lord'. It shall not come to mind, or be remembered, or missed; nor shall another one be made. (Jer 3:16)

Jeremiah indeed foresees the destruction of the temple; and he sees Jerusalem as a spiritual centre for the nations (3:17ff; 7:12-14). Israel will retain its prophetic and priestly role but the nations will respond to God's outreach:

O Lord, my strength and my stronghold, my refuge in the day of trouble, to you shall the nations come from the ends of the earth and say: Our ancestors have inherited nothing but lies, worthless things in which there is no profit. Can mortals make for themselves gods? Such are no gods! (Jer 16:19-20)

Zechariah points to the time when 'the nations that have come against Jerusalem shall go up year after year to worship the King, the Lord of hosts …' (Zech 14:16). Once the nations come, the assembly of the Lord will expand to contain them:

And the foreigners who join themselves to the Lord, to minister to him, to love the name of the Lord, and to be his servants … these I will bring to my holy mountain, and make them joyful in my house of prayer; their burnt offerings and their sacrifices will be accepted on my altar; for my house shall be called a house of prayer for all peoples. (Isa 56:6, 7)

Joel foresees the judgement of God that will assemble all peoples for a definitive reckoning:

Come quickly, all you nations all around, gather yourselves there. ... Let the nations rouse themselves, and come to the valley of Jehoshaphat; for there will I sit to judge all the neighbouring nations. (Joel 3:11–12)

The Deutero-Isaiah expresses the universalist ideas in great language and sees a time not only of the acknowledged reign of God over all peoples but an era of perfect peace:

In days to come the mountain of the Lord's house shall be established as the highest of the mountains, and shall be raised above the hills; all the nations shall stream to it. Many peoples shall come and say, 'Come, let us go up to the mountain of the Lord, to the house of the God of Jacob; that he may teach us his ways and that we may walk in his paths.' ... He shall judge between the nations, and shall arbitrate for many peoples; they shall beat their swords into plowshares, and their spears into pruning hooks; nation shall not lift up sword against nation, neither shall they learn war any more. (Isa 2:2–4)[10]

While some of the traditions that distrusted the kings of the people looked to the direct reign of God, there were other traditions that looked to a messianic king who would in an idealised version of David bring peace and justice, holiness and mercy (Amos 9:11; Hosea 3:5; Jeremiah 30:9; Ezekiel 34:23-24; 37:24). Zechariah looks forward:

> Rejoice greatly, O daughter Zion! Shout aloud, O daughter Jerusalem! Lo, your king comes to you; triumphant and victorious is he, humble and riding on a donkey, on a colt, the foal of a donkey. He will cut off the chariot from Ephraim and the war horse from Jerusalem; and the battle bow shall be cut off, and he shall command peace to the nations; his dominion shall be from sea to sea, and from the River to the ends of the earth. (Zech 9:9-10)

A psalmist in a poem dedicated to Solomon draws a portrait of the ideal king:

> In his days may righteousness flourish and peace abound, until the moon is no more. … May all kings fall down before him, all nations give him service. For he delivers the needy when they call, the poor and those who have no helper. He has pity on the weak and the needy, and saves the lives of the needy. From oppression and violence he redeems their life;

and precious is their blood in his sight. … May
his name endure forever, his fame continue as
long as the sun. May all nations be blessed in
him; may they pronounce him happy.
(Ps 72:7, 11-14, 17)

There is a more obscure depicting of the Messiah
(or of the messianic nation) that emerges in the
second part of Isaiah in hymns referring to the
'Servant of the Lord'. He is anointed by the Lord
but he has no 'stateliness':

> … he had no form or majesty that we should
> look at him, and nothing in his appearance that
> we should desire him. He was despised and
> rejected by others; a man of suffering and
> acquainted with infirmity; and as one from
> whom others hide their faces he was despised,
> and we held him of no account. Surely he has
> borne our infirmities and carried our diseases;
> yet we accounted him stricken, struck down by
> God, and afflicted. But he was wounded for our
> transgressions, crushed for our iniquities; upon
> him was the punishment that made us whole,
> and by his bruises we are healed. All we like
> sheep have gone astray; we have all turned to
> our own way, and the Lord has laid on him the
> iniquity of us all. He was oppressed, and he was
> afflicted, yet he did not open his mouth; like a

lamb that is led to the slaughter, and like a sheep that before its shearers is silent, so he did not open his mouth. By a perversion of justice he was taken away. Who could have imagined his future? For he was cut off from the land of the living, stricken for the transgression of my people. … Yet it was the will of the Lord to crush him with pain. When you make his life an offering for sin, he shall see his offspring, and shall prolong his days; through him the will of the Lord shall prosper. Out of his anguish he shall see light; he shall find satisfaction through his knowledge. The righteous one, my servant, shall make many righteous, and he shall bear their iniquities. (Isa 53:2-11)

But whether or not the era of peace and justice is to bring the direct reign of God or of his messiah-king, in that era the nations will flow towards Jerusalem, and the earlier concept of community that was confined to the Jews is spiritualised and extended. The kingdom of David is on its way to being transformed into the kingdom of heaven.

In short, for the Jews, God is the beginning and the end; he is the God of Israel; and he is holy. It took Jewish religious thinkers and worshippers centuries to work out a rounded understanding of his nature. They believed that this God had offered them an alliance;

and he had made available to them the means through which they could live up to their part of the alliance. While early on they had seen the alliance as a pact with the nation, they had gradually come to grasp that each person had in his or her heart access to God. Finally, they had understood that while the Jews remained privileged witnesses to him, Yahweh was the Lord of the nations. For that reason the nations of the world would have access to the Lord but in some mysterious way they would come through the Jews and Jerusalem. Jesus was to inherit a tradition that he affirmed (John 4:22) and that he would fulfil in ways that were not anticipated by the great majority of his contemporaries; and that many among them found hard to accept. Yet he took the ideas of the prophets and gave them even fuller meaning; he consolidated the universalist mission that the later prophets had begun to grasp; and he founded his church to work for the coming of the kingdom of God.

NOTES

1 Those who want to learn more about the way in which the documents of the Hebrew scriptures were compiled may turn to a good dictionary of the Bible: see, for example, J.L. McKenzie, *Dictionary of the Bible*, New York, 1990.

2 See text of the Fourth Annual E. Maynard Adams Lecture in the Humanities and Human Values, University of North Carolina, Chapel Hill, NC, 23 September 2001: Jack M. Sasson, 'The Search for the Hebrew God', which gives an excellent historical perspective on the development of the idea of God among the Jews.

   http://people.vanderbilt.edu/~jack.m.sasson/Adams_Lecture.htm

3 The manner in which the prophets thunder against the gods and their idols reveals how long and hard the battle was. The dangers came from the need a technologically primitive people felt for putting faces on the powers of the universe, from the nearness of Canaan, and its influences, and not least from the religious and artistic prestige of the Assyrian pantheon. In the time and region of Israel the gods were mostly of four kinds: nature gods, gods of places, occupational gods, and gods of peoples and families. They all made sense of the surroundings of a people and their work; and they gave them a sense of security and protection. There was a supreme god but he was less available to humans; and often he simply presided over a series of dissident gods. It is worth remembering that people in the ancient world were buffeted by nature and constrained within social systems in ways that we cannot easily understand: illness was hard to deal with; distances took a long time to travel; the seasons and crops were unpredictable and famine could readily come; darkness was dangerous and candles and lamps feeble. Those not in authority needed advocates or patrons; families without parents could find themselves in dire straits; and tyranny and injustice could be insuperable. The gods emerged to deal with these things. Not until the one God came to be more fully understood among the Jews did the arbitrariness of the world diminish greatly for them.

4 In the pages that follow on the God of the Old Testament, my portrait of him is obviously a construct from the pages of the scriptures. It is based especially on the concept of God that Jesus and his contemporaries worked with and that Jesus added to. For an excellent and more detailed construct, see Mary E. Mills, *Images of God in the Old Testament*, Collegeville, Mn, 1998.

5 He refers over twenty times to the Holy One of Israel; and he also refers to God as the 'Holy One'.

6 Rabbi Aqaba, who was put to death by the Romans in AD 132, recited the Deuteronomy confession of faith (the first part of the citation in the text) during his execution.

7 Many Hebrew names incorporate the sense of God's fatherhood; to take a few: Abraham means 'father is elevated'; Abiezer: 'father is help'; Abijah: 'Yah(weh) is father'; Joab: 'father is help'; Abitub: 'father is goodness'; Absalom: 'father is peace'.

8 G.M. Hopkins has rewritten this passage in his own poetic style: 'Thou are indeed just, Lord.'

9 *Confessions*, Book I, Chapter 1.

10 See Isaiah 9:9; 19:23–5; 65:17, 18, 25.

III

THE GOD AND FATHER OF JESUS CHRIST

GRACE TO YOU AND PEACE FROM GOD OUR FATHER
AND THE LORD JESUS CHRIST.

EPHESIANS 1:2

In discussing the God of Israel, the previous chapter focused on the understanding of God that the Jews had arrived at around the time of Jesus. In discussing the God and Father of Jesus Christ – a term used three times by St Paul – I want to describe the understanding of God that Christians had come to by the time they had put the New Testament together. Understanding had indeed evolved – and I will take it into consideration – but it had done so in the course of a few short generations of disciples and teachers.

To understand the God of Jesus, three broad approaches are useful. The first is to try to discern the features of God as Jesus and the disciples reveal them – simple but profound descriptions that touch human hearts: God sees, cares and helps. The second approach is to find in Jesus himself the face of God:

who sees me, sees the Father. The third is to understand the work of the incarnation and atonement as the work of God, carried out by and made manifest in Jesus, which lets us understand the God who has willed and accomplished this work for human creatures and sinners.

DESCRIBING GOD: THE FEATURES OF THE FATHER

The Christian writers take up the theme of God's transcendence and power as the prophets had done. Paul refers to:

> ... the King of ages, immortal, invisible, the only God, [to him] be honour and glory for ever and ever. (1 Tim 1:17)

And again:

> ... [the] blessed and only Sovereign, the King of kings and Lord of lords. It is he alone who has immortality and dwells in unapproachable light, whom no one has ever seen or can see ... (1 Tim 6:15-16)

The Apocalypse refers to him:

> ... who lives forever and ever, who created heaven and what is in it, the earth and what is in it, and the sea and what is in it ... (Rev 10:6)

Again its writer puts into the mouth of God:

> 'I am the Alpha and the Omega,' says the Lord

> God, who is and who was and who is to come,
> the Almighty. (Rev 1:8)

Understanding as he did the transcendence of God, when Jesus replied to the tempter who offered him the kingdoms of the world in return for worship, he put the relative worth of things definitively:

> Jesus answered him, 'It is written, "Worship the Lord your God, and serve only him"'. (Lk 4:8)

While insisting on the power of God, time and again Jesus presents this transcendent God gently:

> You have heard that it was said, 'You shall love your neighbour and hate your enemy'. But I say to you, Love your enemies and pray for those who persecute you, so that you may be children of your Father in heaven; for he makes his sun rise on the evil and on the good, and sends rain on the righteous and on the unrighteous. ... Are not two sparrows sold for a penny? Yet not one of them will fall to the ground apart from your Father. And even the hairs of your head are all counted. So do not be afraid; you are of more value than many sparrows. (Mt 5:43-45, 10:29-31)

Jesus in describing the all-knowing God tells at the same time how he cares for all his people:

> … your Father knows what you need before
> you ask him. … Therefore I tell you, do not
> worry about your life, what you will eat or
> what you will drink, or about your body, what
> you will wear. Is not life more than food, and
> the body more than clothing? Look at the birds
> of the air: they neither sow nor reap nor gather
> into barns, and yet your heavenly Father feeds
> them. Are you not of more value than they?
> (Mt 6:8, 25–26)

A most intimate way in which Jesus invites us to
understand God is by his teaching that his Father is
also our Father. In the one prayer that he explicitly
taught his disciples, he said that they should pray:
Our Father in heaven. While the reference to heaven
indicates the transcendence of God, the image of
father and the use of the possessive pronoun ('our')
bring him humanly close to us. It is this God who
clothes the flowers of the fields with beauty and cares
for the small birds; who exercises mercy without
stint; who searches for the son who is lost; who
rewards those who have fed the hungry, visited the
sick and clothed the naked; who listens to the poor
and those deprived of justice; and who welcomes
sinners and rejoices with the angels on the return of
sinners. St Paul, the disciple who had only met Jesus
after the resurrection, describes this God of Jesus:

... the God and Father of our Lord Jesus Christ, the Father of mercies and the God of all consolation, who consoles us in all our affliction, so that we may be able to console those who are in any affliction with the consolation with which we ourselves are consoled by God. (2 Cor 1:3-4)

St John, the beloved disciple, pithily says: 'God is love' (1 Jn 4:7). This is the God who loved us when we were alienated from him; who first loved us before we ever made a move towards him; who so loved the world that he gave to it his only begotten Son; and who in the reconciliation wrought by Christ in a confused and sinful world makes us his children; and so he gives us much more than what creatures could have merited or might even have hoped for.

Yet the Lord's prayer keeps truths in perspective. We are to recognise the spiritual transcendence of God; we ask that the holiness of his name be understood and respected; we ask that his kingdom come; and we ask that his will be done on earth as in heaven. We pray these things before we move on to ask him to provide our daily bread and to keep us out of harm's way. We then offer him a marvellous and dangerous way of forgiving us: we ask him to forgive us as we forgive others. In this request for forgiveness we enter with a similar logic of compassion into the great scene of judgement that Christ describes in which we are judged on what we have done for others, even when we have performed such deeds without consciously adverting that in feeding and healing the needy we were dealing with God (Mt 25:31-45). In short, the God whom Jesus describes is one who cares, seeks and invites, welcomes and listens, provides and forgives, and above all, loves. He wants us, too, to love others, to care for them, and, where need be, to forgive them.

THE FACE OF GOD IN JESUS

St John in the prologue to his gospel introduces the Jesus who is the Word of God and who is God while being also human:

> In the beginning was the Word, and the Word was with God, and the Word was God. He was in the beginning with God. All things came into being through him, and without him not one thing came into being. What has come into being in him was life, and the life was the light of all people. ... He was in the world, and the world came into being through him; yet the world did not know him. He came to what was his own, and his own people did not accept

him. But to all who received him, who
believed in his name, he gave power to become
children of God, who were born, not of blood
or of the will of the flesh or of the will of man,
but of God. And the Word became flesh and
lived among us, and we have seen his glory, the
glory as of a father's only son, full of grace and
truth. (Jn 1:1-4, 10-14)

Jesus insisted that he and the Father were one; and
that all that he said and did came from the Father.
When Philip asked him at the last supper to show the
disciples the Father, Jesus replied: Whoever has seen
me has seen the Father (Jn 14:9).[1] This Jesus is the
person who says that the poor and the peaceful, the
merciful and the pure of heart are blessed; who calls
the weary and hard-pressed to him to give them
comfort; who forgives sins where there is love and
repentance; who says that if you are hit on one cheek,
you need to turn the other, to let your cloak go with
a thief as well as your other garment, and to walk a
step further on the road than what somebody is
unreasonably compelling you to do; who invites a
rich young man to leave everything and to follow
him; who takes the law of the sabbath into the higher
law of human needs; who sets aside the precepts of
Moses and tradition because he inaugurates the reign
of God; who washes his disciples' feet to assert the

role of service; who insists that people will recognise the disciples by the love that they have for one another; and who sums up the Law and the prophets in saying that they mean love of God and neighbour.

It is this Jesus too who shows how God avoids the psychological threat to many humans that his greatness poses by becoming a small and dependent child; who says that his prophetic ministry was inspired by the Holy Spirit (Mt 12:28); whose baptism by John was his messianic anointing by the Spirit (Mk 1:10-11); who walks the tracks and hills of Galilee, sits tired by the well in Samaria, and yet uses the opportunity to open up the mind and touch the heart of an unrespectable woman (Jn 4); who calls the outcasts and sinners to him; who forgives sins; who confronts the religious and secular authorities in carrying out his mission and defies their power; who shows fear at Gethsemane and anguish on the cross but who obeys his Father and carries on his mission to the end; who in some strange way survives the crucifixion; and who while leaving the Spirit behind to continue his work goes away to be with the Father.

After the resurrection the nature and activity of the Paraclete are similar to those of Jesus before his glorification but he is distinguished from Jesus:

And I will ask the Father, and he will give you another Advocate, to be with you forever. This is the Spirit of truth, whom the world cannot receive, because it neither sees him nor knows him. You know him, because he abides with you, and he will be in you. ... But the Advocate, the Holy Spirit, whom the Father will send in my name, will teach you everything and remind you of all that I have said to you. ... When the Spirit of truth comes, he will guide you into all the truth; for he will not speak on his own, but will speak whatever he hears, and he will declare to you the things that are to come. He will glorify me, because he will take what is mine and declare it to you. All that the Father has is mine. For this reason I said that he will take what is mine and declare it to you. (Jn 14:16–17, 26; 16:13–14)

With this teaching and promise Jesus spiritualises the faith and community that he leaves behind: God is to be worshipped in spirit and in truth. We are sent back to the scene at Jacob's well:

Jesus said to her, 'Woman, believe me, the hour is coming when you will worship the father neither on this mountain nor in Jerusalem. You worship what you do not know; we worship what we know, for salvation is from the Jews.

> But the hour is coming, and is now here, when
> the true worshippers will worship the Father in
> spirit and truth, for the Father seeks such as
> these to worship him. God is spirit, and those
> who worship him must worship in spirit and
> truth.' (Jn 4:21-24)

Jesus distinguishes the Spirit from both himself and
the Father, and yet God remains one.

It is the human identity of Jesus that associates
him with us and enables him to represent us:

> Therefore he had to become like his brothers
> and sisters in every respect, so that he might be
> a merciful and faithful high priest in the service
> of God, to make a sacrifice of atonement for
> the sins of the people. Because he himself was
> tested by what he suffered, he is able to help
> those who are being tested. ... we do not have
> a high priest who is unable to sympathise with
> our weaknesses, but we have one who in every
> respect has been tested as we are, yet without
> sin. (Heb 2:17-18; 4:15)

It is however the divine identity that he asserts that
gives a peculiar worth, beyond human worth, to the
work that he undertook in this world on behalf of
us, sinful humans. In a much more elaborate way
than the simple sentence in which Jesus told Philip

that he who saw him saw the Father, the Epistle to the Hebrews sets out a theology of sonship:

> Long ago God spoke to our ancestors in many and various ways by the prophets, but in these last days he has spoken to us by a Son, whom he appointed heir of all things, through whom he also created the worlds. He is the reflection of God's glory and the exact imprint of God's very being, and he sustains all things by his powerful word. (Heb 1:1-3)

St Paul, in writing to the Corinthians, describes with an economy of words the roles of the Father and Jesus:

> … for us there is one God, the Father, from whom are all things and for whom we exist, and one Lord, Jesus Christ, through whom are all things and through whom we exist.
> (1 Cor 8:6)

In a more elaborate way the writer to the Colossians not only describes the divine role of Jesus but links it with his work of redemption:

> He is the image of the invisible God, the firstborn of all creation; for in him all things on heaven and on earth were created, things visible and invisible, whether thrones or dominions or rulers or powers – all things have been created

through him and for him. He himself is before all things, and in him all things hold together. He is the head of the body, the church; he is the beginning, the first-born from the dead, so that he might come to have first place in everything. For in him all the fullness of God was pleased to dwell, and through him God was pleased to reconcile to himself all things, whether on earth or in heaven, by making peace through the blood of his cross. (Col 1:15-20)

Jesus on our behalf shared and transformed the tragedy of human suffering and took it into a scheme in which glory would crown the suffering.

If you endure what you are beaten for doing wrong, what credit is that? But if you endure when you do right and suffer for it, you have God's approval. For to this you have been called, because Christ also suffered for you, leaving you an example, so that you should follow in his steps. 'He committed no sin, and no deceit was found in his mouth.' When he was abused, he did not return abuse; when he suffered, he did not threaten; but he entrusted himself to the one who judges justly. He himself bore our sins in his body on the cross, so that, free from sins, we might live for righteousness; by his wounds you have been healed. (1 Pet 2:20-24)

This Jesus is the Word made flesh; he is one with the Father; he embodies the presence of God in his work; and he sets the example for us of the purification that is needed to make our way to God.

THE WORK OF THE FATHER

There are three crucial actions of God in the New Covenant. First, in loving the world, God, the heavenly Father, sends his Son into the world to save it from its sinfulness. Second, he accepts that his Son in a sinful world will be rejected, humiliated and made to suffer. Third, he justifies the work of this Son by raising him from the dead; and in that act also offers us forgiveness, sets up reconciliation, and gives the hope of resurrection. All three actions are conveyed in the salient text:

> For God so loved the world that he gave his only Son, so that everyone who believes in him may not perish but may have eternal life. (Jn 3:16)

In all love there is a moment of giving that transcends utility and that precedes reciprocity. Such love is conveyed in one of the loveliest passages in scripture: 'In this is love, not that we loved God but that he loved us and sent his Son to be the atoning sacrifice for our sins' (1 Jn 4:10).

Love also is judged by the sacrifices that are made for the beloved:

> He who did not withhold his own Son, but gave him up for all of us, will he not with him also give us everything else? (Rom 8:32)

There was great cost in sending his Son. Jesus came to reconcile a sinful humanity with his – and our – Father and he would inevitably suffer in carrying out his Father's mission and working for our sake. He was to humble himself, even to the death of the cross. Since it is more important to say that we had estranged ourselves from God than he was estranged from us, Paul, in writing to the Romans, draws attention to the love of God for us when we were unreconciled with him:

> … God's love has been poured into our hearts through the Holy Spirit that has been given to us. For while we were still weak, at the right time Christ died for the ungodly. Indeed, rarely will anyone die for a righteous person – though perhaps for a good person someone might actually dare to die. But God proves his love for us in that while we were sinners Christ died for us. Much more surely then, now that we have been justified by his blood, will we be saved through him from the wrath of God. For if while we were enemies, we were reconciled

> to God through the death of his Son, much more surely, having been reconciled, will we be saved by his life. But more than that, we even boast in God through our Lord Jesus Christ, through whom we have now received reconciliation. (Rom 5:5-11)

The complicated theology of the passage from Paul was put in simple language by Peter in one of the earliest expositions of the Christian message to a Jewish audience:

> The God of our ancestors raised up Jesus, whom you had killed by hanging him on a tree. God exalted him at his right hand as Leader and Saviour that he might give repentance to Israel and forgiveness of sins. (Acts 5:30-32)

If Paul expands on reconciliation and Peter emphasises how God confirmed the worth of the work of Jesus by raising him from the dead, later Christian writers develop in other ways the central themes of the life, death and resurrection of Christ. Hebrews, for example, readily sees Jesus' suffering in the tradition of the prophets and states the implications for our lives:

> ... Jesus also suffered outside the city gate in order to sanctify the people by his own blood.

> Let us then go to him outside the camp and
> bear the abuse he endured. (Heb 13:12-13)

Yet the main thrust of Hebrews is to set Jesus in the priestly tradition and to explain his work of mediation:

> … 'The Lord has sworn and will not change his
> mind, "You are a priest for ever"' – accordingly
> Jesus has also become the guarantee of a better
> covenant. Furthermore, the former priests were
> many in number, because they were prevented
> by death from continuing in office; but he
> holds his priesthood permanently, because he
> continues forever. Consequently he is able for
> all time to save those who approach God
> through him, since he always lives to make
> intercession for them. (Heb 7:21-25)

In a broader sweep again, and in powerful language, the prologue to the Ephesians spells the relationship of creation and atonement:

> Blessed be the God and Father of our Lord
> Jesus Christ, who has blessed us in Christ with
> every spiritual blessing in the heavenly places,
> just as he chose us in Christ before the
> foundation of the world to be holy and
> blameless before him in love. He destined us for
> adoption as his children through Jesus Christ,

according to the good pleasure of his will, to the praise of his glorious grace that he freely bestowed on us in the Beloved. In him we have redemption through his blood, the forgiveness of our trespasses, according to the riches of his grace that he lavished on us. With all wisdom and insight he has made known to us the mystery of his will, according to his good pleasure that he set forth in Christ, as a plan for the fullness of time, to gather up all things in him, things in heaven and things on earth. (Eph 1:3-10)

St John in referring to the advocacy of Christ with the Father returns again to a simple theology of the atonement and holds out practical hope for those who will never be perfect:

… if anyone does sin, we have an advocate with the Father, Jesus Christ the righteous; and he is the atoning sacrifice for our sins, and not for ours only but also for the sins of the whole world. (1 Jn 2:1-2)

The work of God that culminated in raising Jesus from the dead and placing him at the right hand of the Father has come about because God so loved the world as to send his only Son into the world to save sinful humans. In raising Jesus, God raised in principle all those with whom he shared a human nature and whom he represented. All have become children of God and the brothers and sisters of Jesus. Far beyond what reason might have suggested for humans and more even than the Fatherhood of God promised in the Hebrew scriptures, those who have put on Christ enter into a new intimacy with God and hold a claim on his inheritance.

The profoundest word to describe the work of God is at-one-ment, which the prologue to Ephesians expresses so well. But the atonement is built on a reconciliation of humans with God and the forgiveness of sins. As the atonement takes place, the result for humans is not simply the taking away of guilt and the remission of punishment but a new status that is given to the redeemed. If the simplest and most human description of Christians is as the adopted, yet real, children of God, New Testament writers offer also a further variety of descriptions for the new state of human kind: they have become members of Christ, members of a body of which Christ is the head; they share in the divine nature; they are described as the disciples and friends of Jesus; they are, not least, the people of God, a phrase that occurs several times in scripture but that in one of the Petrine letters is flanked by other descriptions of those chosen by God:

> … you are a chosen race, a royal priesthood, a holy nation, God's own people, in order that you may proclaim the mighty acts of him who called you out of darkness into his marvellous light. (1 Pet 2:9)

To end this section on the work of the Father we may reflect that those who are loved take in good measure their sense of worth from whoever loves them. To know that we were so loved by God when we were sinners, and that God gave up for us his Son, imparts to us who are still conscious of finitude and sin a worth and a strength that have their roots in God and that share in God's glory and power. Such love invites our love in return, which we express not only in loving God but in loving our neighbour. We are not promised easefulness as we love but in the purification of love face the suffering symbolised by the cross. But the promise is that if we suffer with Christ, then we shall live with him in the company of God.

NOTE

1 All the chapters in John 14–17 take up this theme from one perspective or another.

CONCLUSION

In considering the God of the philosophers, the God of the Jews, and the God and Father of Jesus Christ, I have limited myself to reflecting in a relatively simple way on the nature and the work of God. For that reason I have only begun to do justice to the complexity of natural theology, to the varied riches of the Hebrew scriptures, to the wonderful analyses and images of the Christian scriptures, and to the subtle and sympathetic descriptions of the person of Jesus in the gospels.

In ending I want nevertheless to make some fundamental points. In the introduction I suggested that few would come to know and fewer still be willing to die for the God of philosophers. Aquinas in the opening to his *Summa Theologica* stresses as a theologian the intellectual considerations in the limits of philosophy.

> Even as regards those truths about God which human reason could have discovered, it was necessary that man should be taught by a divine revelation; because the truth about God such as reason could discover, would only be known by a few, and that after a long time, and with the admixture of many errors …

> Therefore, in order that the salvation of men might be brought about more fitly and more surely, it was necessary that they should be taught divine truths by divine revelation. It was therefore necessary that besides philosophical science built up by reason, there should be a sacred science learned through revelation.[1]

A God of faith who was much richer in recognisable features and more accessible than the God of reason could reach out not only to the philosophers but to the whole of humankind. God fortunately for us intervened in history through the Jewish founders and the prophets and, finally, through his Son to make himself accessible to us, to enable us to overcome our sins, and to create a community through which the good news of the kingdom would go on being transmitted. Many thoughtful and courageous people have been willing to die to uphold the truth of God's intervention and to return his love.

Second, through the life and death of Jesus, the Father joined together the reign of God and the coming of the Messiah or the Christ. Moreover, the kingdom of God, which the prophets had seen as opening up to the gentiles, was opened up definitively by Jesus who ordered his disciples to preach to all nations and who said that peoples would come from the east and the west to sit down in the kingdom with the children of Abraham. He established a new community, the Church, that was entered through faith and baptism, that began with the Jews and then reached out to the whole world. Jesus avoided the rigours of the Law and its ritual and historical narrowness by teaching that the requirements of the Law and the prophets were summed up in the double commandment of love of God and neighbours; and he bequeathed the Spirit as an advocate through whom his disciples had the maturity that enabled the works of the Law to be dispensed with.[2] He embodied in his own person the priestly functions of the Temple; and he left a sacred meal to his followers as the central commemoration of him and his sacrificial work.

In a word, the final gesture of the Father is to accept the life of the Son whom he had sent into the world and the lives of all of us who through the Spirit have shared that life, death and resurrection. Two final visions, one tentative and nuanced, and the other clothed in prophetic dress, sum up a Christian apocalypse that reaches beyond time. First, St John's letter, while acknowledging that many had rejected Jesus, reaches towards the final vision of God:

> See what love the Father has given us, that we
> should be called children of God; and that is
> what we are. The reason the world does not

> know us is that it did not know him. Beloved, we are God's children now; what we will be has not yet been revealed. What we do know is this: when he is revealed, we will be like him, for we will see him as he is. And all who have this hope in him purify themselves, just as he is pure. (1 Jn 3:1-3)

Second, the ultimate scenario in Revelation offers a vision of a purified Church that through the gift of the eternal God enjoys happiness without flaw or end:

> Then I saw a new heaven and a new earth; for the first heaven and the first earth had passed away, and the sea was no more. And I saw the holy city, the new Jerusalem, coming down out of heaven from God, prepared as a bride adorned for her husband; and I heard a loud voice from the throne saying, 'See, the home of God is among mortals. He will dwell with them as their God; they will be his peoples, and God himself will be with them; he will wipe every tear from their eyes. Death will be no more; mourning and crying and pain will be no more, for the first things have passed away. ... I am the Alpha and the Omega, the beginning and the end. ... (Rev 21:1-4, 6)

Third, it is crucial to return constantly to the understanding of God that comes through the prophets, and especially the understanding that comes through the teaching and person of Jesus. In spite of the clarity of the teaching and the saliency and gentleness of Jesus, believers have time and again forged an image of God that derived excessively from their particular historical circumstances and that diminished the God who is love.[3] Yet at all times there have been those who have read the scriptures carefully, prayed the Eucharist in a spirit of reconciliation, and enabled those around them to discern the features of the God of love, compassion, forgiveness and reconciliation. The search for the true God has to go on unceasingly; and we need to join with those who best portray this God.

NOTES

1 *Summa Theologica*, Prima Pars, Q. 1.

2 The Law itself was made up of moral precepts that emphasised social and personal integrity, legal precepts on behaviour that underpinned order, and various practices common to the peoples of the time as well as customs and prohibitions that distinguished the Jews from other peoples and held them together as a people. Those early Jewish Christians of the diaspora with whom Paul (and Peter) came into some conflict cherished the works of the Law (circumcision, food taboos and other practices) because they saw them as a cherished part of their God-given heritage and a support for their distinctiveness as a people. Paul realised that retaining the works of the Law would limit the appeal of the faith of Jesus among the gentiles; and he argued that to maintain the distinctiveness that those works had earlier fostered, Christians now had the new strength that had come from Christ.

The Law had a pedagogic role during difficult centuries but Christ had in the maturity of time set his people free from the constraints of the Law.

3   An Irish priest-novelist, Canon P.A. Sheehan, in *Luke Delmege* has a young priest dealing with an old tenant farmer on his deathbed. The final question that the old man, after receiving the last rites, puts to the young priest is whether the 'Man above' has anything now against him in his books. The young man realises that God is being envisaged as a powerful landlord.